LOCAL GOVERNMENT COMMISSION
FOR ENGLAND

THE FUTURE LOCAL GOVERNMENT OF COUNTY DURHAM

SECOND REVIEW: DRAFT RECOMMENDATIONS

A REPORT TO LOCAL RESIDENTS

London: HMSO

THE LOCAL GOVERNMENT COMMISSION FOR ENGLAND

This report sets out the draft recommendations for local government in County Durham agreed by the Commission:

Sir John Banham (Chairman)
David Ansbro*
Professor Michael Chisholm
Christopher Chope OBE
Sir Kenneth Couzens KCB
Kenneth Ennals CB
Professor Malcolm Grant
Brian Hill CBE DL
Miss Mary Leigh
Mrs Ann Levick*
Robert Scruton
David Thomas
Lady Judith Wilcox
Clive Wilkinson

Martin Easteal (Chief Executive)

*Lead Commissioners for this review

Local Government Commission for England

Sir John Banham
Chairman

FOREWORD FROM THE CHAIRMAN

Dear Resident,

The Local Government Commission has been directed to look again at its earlier recommendations to the Secretary of State for the Environment on the future structure, boundaries and electoral arrangements of local government in County Durham.

The Commission wishes to see a structure which reflects local loyalties and community interests, offers clear democratic accountability to local people, and delivers effective management and use of resources over time. Our earlier recommendations included the proposal that a unitary authority be established for Darlington and that the two-tier system remains in the rest of the county. It remains the Commission's view that this is the best structure for County Durham at this time.

We would like to know the views of the people of County Durham before submitting a further report to the Secretary of State for the Environment. You can let us have your views by writing directly to the Commission at the address set out in paragraph 86 on page 31.

I should stress that the draft recommendations in this report do not prejudge our final recommendations. These will be prepared in the light of the local reaction to this report. As there is no national blueprint to be imposed on local communities, we treat each area on its merits. That is why your views are important.

We would like to have your views no later than 26 September 1994 so that we can consider them properly before submitting our final report to the Secretary of State. We very much look forward to hearing from you.

Yours sincerely

Sir John Banham
Chairman, Local Government Commission for England
12 July 1994

CONTENTS

1 BACKGROUND TO THE REPORT

1 The Local Government Act of 1992 established the Local Government Commission for England as an independent body. Its main tasks are to examine the structure of local government in the English shire counties to determine whether the existing two-tier structure of county and district councils should be replaced by a structure of all-purpose 'unitary' authorities, and to review boundary and electoral arrangements throughout England. The Commission is required to make recommendations – either for change or for no change – to the Secretary of State for the Environment.

2 The Commission is required by the Act to have regard to the need to reflect the identities and interests of local communities and the need to secure effective and convenient local government. The Commission is also required to have regard to guidance that has been issued by the Government on the policy considerations that should be taken into account and on the procedures that should be followed. Copies of the guidance, which is extensive and has been the subject of detailed discussion between the Government and representatives of local authorities, are available from the Commission or the Department of the Environment.

3 The review of Durham and Cleveland was originally launched on 14 September 1992. In Stage 2, starting on 30 November 1992, the Commission prepared its draft recommendations, which were set out in a consultation report, *The Future Local Government of Cleveland and Durham*, published on 10 May 1993. Stage 3 comprised an unprecedented consultation programme on these draft recommendations. In Stage 4 the Commission considered all the evidence in preparing recommendations to the Secretary of State which were published on 8 November 1993 in the report, *Final Recommendations on the Future Local Government in Cleveland and Durham*.

4 The Commission was subsequently directed by the Secretary of State to undertake a second review of County Durham. This report sets out the Commission's draft recommendations for County Durham in the light of the statutory requirements. Many of the issues dealt with here are common to most local government in England. While accepting that there should be no single blueprint for the structure throughout England, the Commission has carefully considered many of the general issues involved and has set out its conclusions in its report, *Renewing Local Government in the English Shires*, published in December 1993 (and available from HMSO).

5 The Commission is required to review the administrative units of local government: county, district and borough *councils*. There is no question of the abolition of historic County Durham, whatever may be recommended in the way of the structure of local government in the county or the future of the county council. The Commission recognises that many people have strongly held loyalties to their county areas, which have long and valued histories. Historic County Durham will continue as a focus for loyalty and identity, as well as for historic, ceremonial and other

Map 1

THE EXISTING LOCAL GOVERNMENT STRUCTURE IN COUNTY DURHAM

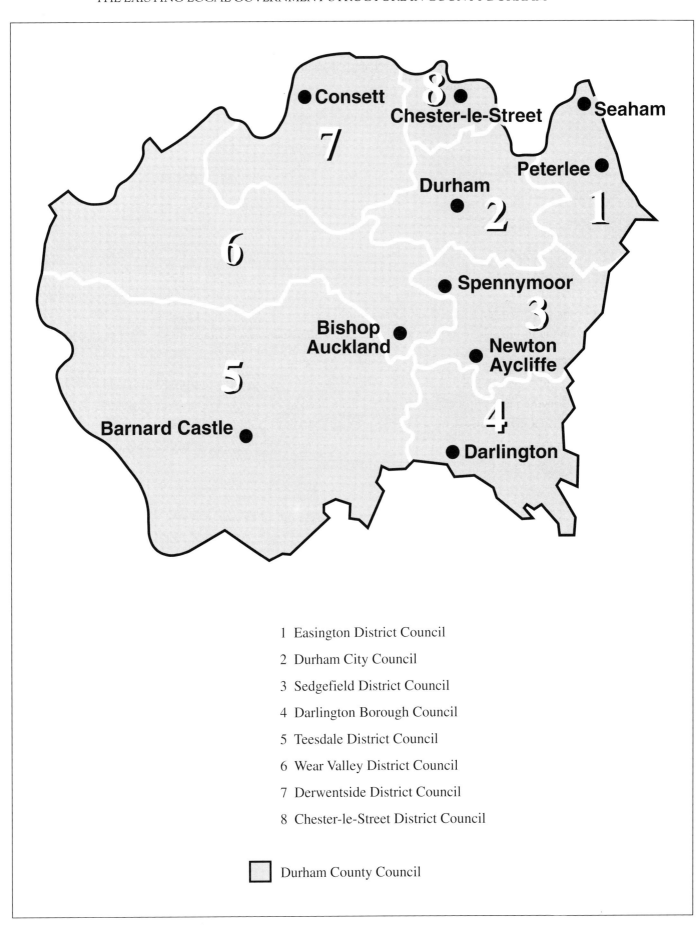

1 Easington District Council

2 Durham City Council

3 Sedgefield District Council

4 Darlington Borough Council

5 Teesdale District Council

6 Wear Valley District Council

7 Derwentside District Council

8 Chester-le-Street District Council

Durham County Council

purposes. It can also continue to be an appropriate unit for voluntary and sporting organisations and indeed for local government collaboration.

6 The Commission has not been invited to consider the role of local government, how it should be financed, or the internal management arrangements for local authorities. However, research and prospective changes in each of these has been taken into account by the Commission.

THE PRESENT LOCAL GOVERNMENT STRUCTURE IN COUNTY DURHAM

7 Local government in the county comprises one county council and eight district councils. The eight district councils shown in map 1 range from the remote rural districts of Teesdale and Wear Valley dominated by the high Pennines, to the more industrial areas of mid and east Durham. The county was a former palatinate ruled by the prince bishops and this rich heritage is particularly evident in Durham City which has been designated a world heritage site.

8 The county was dominated by the iron and coal industries and their decline has created serious challenges for local government in regenerating the area. The former county borough of Darlington developed with the advent of the railways. Road and rail links are good north and south, with major railway stations at Durham and Darlington. Transport links between Darlington and Teesside are also good, but elsewhere east-west links are weaker.

Figure 1
LOCAL AUTHORITIES IN COUNTY DURHAM

Authority	Population	Area (ha)	Population density (pop/ha)
Chester-le-Street	52,900	6,800	7.8
Darlington	100,100	19,800	5.1
Derwentside	87,200	27,100	3.2
Durham City	87,800	19,000	4.6
Easington	99,400	14,300	7.0
Sedgefield	91,700	21,700	4.2
Teesdale	24,300	84,200	0.3
Wear Valley	63,600	50,500	1.3
Durham County Council	607,100	243,400	2.5

Sources: OPCS mid-1992 estimates for population figures; Municipal Yearbook 1994 for area.

Figure 2
SUMMARY OF LOCAL AUTHORITIES' CURRENT FUNCTIONS

County Council	District Councils
EDUCATION * Most schools * Special education * Nursery, adult and community * Planning and quality assurance * Resource management	ELECTORAL REGISTRATION COUNCIL TAX AND UNIFORM BUSINESS RATE COLLECTION
PERSONAL SOCIAL SERVICES * Securing provision for the elderly, children and those with disabilities (including care in the community) * Policy planning and quality assurance	HOUSING * Management and maintenance of housing stock, policy and co-ordination, homelessness.
POLICE	
FIRE	
PLANNING * Strategic planning * Mineral and waste planning * Highway development control * Historic buildings	PLANNING * Local plans * Planning applications
TRANSPORT * Public transport * Highways and parking * Traffic management * Footpaths and bridleways * Transport planning	TRANSPORT * Unclassified roads * Offstreet car parking * Footpaths and bridleways * Street lighting
EMERGENCY PLANNING	EMERGENCY PLANNING
ENVIRONMENTAL SERVICES * Refuse disposal	ENVIRONMENTAL SERVICES * Refuse collection * Building regulations * General environmental services * Street cleaning
RECREATION AND ART * Parks and open spaces * Support for the arts * Museums * Encouraging tourism	RECREATION AND ART * Parks and open spaces * Leisure centres and swimming pools * Support for the arts * Museums and art galleries * Encouraging tourism
ECONOMIC DEVELOPMENT	ECONOMIC DEVELOPMENT
SMALL HOLDINGS	ALLOTMENTS
REGISTRATION * Birth, deaths and marriages	CEMETERIES AND CREMATORIA
CONSUMER PROTECTION * Trading standards etc. * Public analysis	
LIBRARIES	
COUNTY AND DISTRICT EMPLOYEES' PENSIONS (administering authority)	= shared responsibility

9   The range of local services, and their division between the county council and the district councils, is shown in figure 2. Local authorities in England are responsible for a wider range of services than is the case in many other countries but the range of services is subject to change. For example, responsibility for further education has recently been removed from local government while new responsibilities for providing care in the community have been added.

10   The county council accounts for almost two-thirds of gross local government spending in the county. This reflects the responsibilities of the county council which include education and social services. Local taxation (Council Tax) is expected generally to raise less than 20 per cent of gross expenditure. The provision of rented housing accounts for a large proportion of district council gross spending. A breakdown of expenditure in 1993/94 is set out in figure 3 below.

Figure 3
LOCAL AUTHORITY REVENUE EXPENDITURE 1993/94

Authority	Net Revenue Expenditure (£million)	Gross Revenue Expenditure (£million)
Chester-le-Street	5	23
Darlington	12	45
Derwentside	11	49
Durham City	8	34
Easington	11	58
Sedgefield	11	36
Teesdale	2	4
Wear Valley	8	36
Durham County Council	366	492
Total for review area	434	777

Source: Council Tax leaflets, 1993/94
Note: Net revenue expenditure is gross revenue expenditure (the total amount spent by councils) less government grants, rents, fees and other charges.

11   The pattern of local authority responsibilities and spending is reflected in the staffing of authorities. The county council employs by far the largest number of staff, many of them providing services directly in schools, libraries, social services offices and other delivery points across the county. The county council employs almost three-quarters of the total local government employees (full time equivalents) in the county area. Figure 4 shows the staffing levels for the county council and each of the districts.

Figure 4

STAFFING NUMBERS (FULL TIME EQUIVALENTS) 31 March 1994

Authority	Staffing Numbers
Chester-le-Street	500
Darlington	1,000
Derwentside	1,000
Durham City	1,100
Easington	1,300
Sedgefield	900
Teesdale	100
Wear Valley	500
Durham County Council	18,400
Total for review area	24,800

Source: Council Tax leaflets, 1993/94

THE CASE FOR UNITARY AUTHORITIES

12 The case for unitary government has from the outset enjoyed the full support of the three main political parties in England. It has also been supported by many local authorities. All see unitary local government as providing the opportunity for a wholly new approach to the management and delivery of local services.

13 For its part, the Government believes that unitary authorities can reduce bureaucracy and costs and improve the co-ordination and quality of services, but does not wish to impose a national blueprint. This is a view shared by the Commission. While each county review area must be considered on its own merits, having regard to its own particular characteristics, including the identities and interests of its local communities, in the Commission's view a unitary structure may offer substantial advantages for local people in many areas. The main arguments in support are set out below.

(i) **The needs of the consumer.** The effective provision of public services requires an emphasis on the needs of local people. There can be benefits in a combined and co-ordinated approach, for example, between housing and social services, or leisure and education. At present these services are provided by two different local government organisations, sometimes with differing priorities. The present structure is confusing and difficult for people to understand. It can be more effective as well as more comprehensible to local people if the full range of services is planned and delivered by a single authority in a co-ordinated way. The opportunity is there for better services, more convenient to the user as well as more cost effective.

(ii) **The needs of the local community.** The division of functions between the two tiers of local government can create a loss of accountability to the local electorate by county and district councillors. A particular problem arises from the system of local tax collection, whereby the district councils collect all the local tax while the county council is responsible for the expenditure of most of the money simply because of the nature of the services it must provide.

(iii) **Efficiency and effectiveness.** If the creation of unitary authorities is accompanied by a reduction in the total number of authorities, there should be a reduction over time in central administration costs and overheads within local authorities, although the Commission is cautious about claims for substantial cost savings arising from any reorganisation. Nevertheless, a better focus of effort and the elimination of overlap, combined with management within a single organisation, should produce savings.

14   The establishment of unitary authorities does not itself eliminate the risk that councils might become remote or fail to serve local people well. New authorities of whatever size and structure will need to adopt devolved management arrangements and be close to their consumers so that they respond to what local people really want. There will also be a need for constant vigilance by councillors to ensure that efficiency and effectiveness do improve. Specifically, the Commission endorses positive moves to decentralise management. This would enable services to be managed locally within communities to the greatest extent possible, ensuring that information and advice on local government services are readily available in each community and that any enquiries or complaints are speedily addressed. The Commission also hopes that a closer relationship will evolve between the new authorities and parish and town councils, perhaps along the lines of a 'local charter'. There needs at least to be a full opportunity for consultation on important local issues.

THE CASE FOR THE RETENTION OF A TWO-TIER STRUCTURE

15   The Commission does not think that the benefits of unitary authorities only apply to large urban areas. It is no doubt the case, however, that in a single city or major town with a large population it is easier to reconcile the requirements of community identity and service effectiveness. It is also easier to visualise the benefits to be gained from the management of related services in a compact area. These benefits may not be so obvious or clear cut in rural areas, or in areas with no major towns. The task of the Commission is therefore to balance the criteria of community identity, service effectiveness and cost efficiency in determining the appropriateness of unitary authorities in any review area.

16   However, even with devolved service delivery and local consultation, a large unitary authority in a rural/small town situation may be perceived as being too remote and unresponsive to local needs. The strength of the two-tier structure is that it provides the framework in which services that require a strategic view are handled by the

county council, while the district councils cater for more local needs and are able to represent these to the county council as and when appropriate. It also minimises the need for joint arrangements, voluntary or otherwise, for the effective delivery of services, which can be a consequence of changing to a unitary structure of local government. Given the need to reconcile convenient and effective local government with the identities and interests of local communities, it may be that a two-tier structure in some areas is the most suitable form of local government.

17 The Commission is not sitting in judgement on the performance of individual authorities or groups of authorities. However, it may be relevant to its task if it finds that a particular structure, especially one with exceptional elements of successful delegation or co-operation, has shown itself to work particularly well, and is linked with other factors tending to the retention of a two-tier system, as rehearsed in these paragraphs.

*   *   *

18 In its work so far, the Commission has generally adopted the view, subject to particular local circumstances and the principles set out in its report, *Renewing Local Government in the English Shires*, that major cities and towns with a relatively high population density are good candidates for unitary status, perhaps based upon existing district councils' areas, while areas of low population density should either be served by larger unitary authorities or retain the existing two-tier system. However, the Commission does not seek to impose a national blueprint and looks carefully at the particular characteristics and needs of each county area.

2 THE VIEWS EXPRESSED TO THE COMMISSION

19 The Secretary of State issued a Direction on 27 November 1993 directing the Commission to conduct a further review of County Durham under his revised Policy and Procedure Guidance (November 1993) and to make revised recommendations. This second review commenced on 13 December 1993.

20 At the start of the second review, members of the public and all interested parties were invited to write to the Commission giving their views on the future local government of County Durham. The Commissioners with particular responsibility for the review in County Durham, Ann Levick and David Ansbro, have met local authority members and officers, interest groups and individuals. During Stage 2, which began on 30 April 1994, the Commission has considered both the earlier evidence presented during the original review and the new evidence submitted since 13 December 1993.

21 Durham County Council commissioned a survey in 1992 by Market & Opinion Research International (MORI) to examine local perceptions of community identity. The survey, similar to those commissioned directly by the Commission, covered interviews with 1,411 residents aged 18 and over and was conducted between 13 June and 17 July 1992. This research was published in July 1992 and a copy of the report may be obtained from MORI, price £10.

22 The results of the Commission's public consultation exercise on its draft recommendations from its first review of County Durham are shown in figure 5. A total of nearly 28,000 residents expressed their views directly to the Commission. In notable contrast, fewer than 100 representations were received during Stage 1 of the second review. The majority endorsed the Commission's recommendation to the Secretary of State. Others questioned the need for a second review. Concern was voiced by business organisations that Darlington ought to be considered as part of County Durham, rather than looking to the Teesside sub-region, for economic development activities. Little support was expressed for unitary structures outside Darlington.

Figure 5

RESIDENTS' VIEWS EXPRESSED DIRECT TO THE COMMISSION ON THE
DRAFT RECOMMENDATIONS IN THE FIRST REVIEW

Preferred local government structure	Number	Percentage
Status quo	13,903	(49.9%)
Two unitary authorities (Darlington and rest of county)	8,074	(29.0%)
Eight unitary authorities	3,444	(12.4%)
One unitary authority	920	(3.3%)
Four unitary authorities (Darlington; Easington; Chester-le-Street, Derwentside and Durham City; and Sedgefield, Teesdale and Wear Valley)	257	(0.9%)
Other	1,269	(4.5%)
TOTAL	27,867	(100%)

Source: Local Government Commission, November 1993

23   In addition to the guidance from the Government, the Commission has received a
     wide spectrum of views from national organisations with a particular interest in the
     issues raised by local government reorganisation. Almost unanimously those
     favouring change have recommended unitary authorities larger than the existing
     districts; but there has also been considerable support for the retention of the existing
     two-tier structure. Each of the local authorities in County Durham has also let the
     Commission know its views.

RESIDENTS' ATTITUDES TO CHANGE

24   Local attitudes to change are important. It has generally been the Commission's
     experience that, in principle, residents favour a unitary system of local government.
     However, there are some review areas (particularly County Durham) where support
     for such a system has proved to be weak. Furthermore, we have also found that when
     residents are given choices for unitary structures it can be difficult to translate support
     for the unitary principle into support for actual unitary structures.

25   As part of its market research on community identity in County Durham, the
     Commission sought the views of local residents on unitary authorities, full details of
     which appear in MORI's report, *Durham Residents Stage 3 Survey*, published in
     October 1993.

26   On balance, and alone among the areas that the Commission has so far reviewed,
     Durham residents are opposed to the principle of unitary authorities replacing the
     present two-tier structure: 39 per cent support the principle while 47 per cent oppose.
     Support exceeded opposition in Darlington (74 per cent versus 18 per cent) and
     Easington (52 per cent versus 35 per cent). Figure 6 sets out the results by district.

Figure 6

SUPPORT FOR THE PRINCIPLE OF UNITARY LOCAL GOVERNMENT

Question: 'Please tell me whether you support or oppose the following proposal. One council should provide services for this area, rather than the present county council and district council'

Percentage of respondents

District	Support	Oppose	Neither/ no opinion
Chester-le-Street	23	56	21
Darlington	74	18	8
Derwentside	21	67	12
Durham City	37	47	16
Easington	52	35	13
Sedgefield	30	55	15
Teesdale	35	56	9
Wear Valley	21	66	13
Overall	39	47	14

Source: MORI, October 1993

THE IDENTITIES AND INTERESTS OF LOCAL COMMUNITIES

27   The Commission considered it helpful to establish baseline information on the priorities people attach to the various factors that will influence local government structure. MORI was commissioned to survey public opinion throughout the areas of England subject to review.

28   This survey enabled the Commission to gauge the relative importance the public gives to major factors that will influence government structure. The responses to the question 'Which three of these factors, if any, do you think should be more important in deciding the local government structure in your area?' are shown in figure 7. The survey reveals that quality of services and responsiveness to local people score most highly in people's concerns; conversely, historic or traditional boundaries do not figure as a priority consideration.

Figure 7

FACTORS DETERMINING LOCAL GOVERNMENT STRUCTURE

Percentage of respondents mentioning each factor

Quality of services	64
Responding to local people's wishes	58
Cost of services	44
Accountability	36
Ease of contacting the council	20
Sense of local community	18
Access to local councillors	18
Level of information about the council and its services	16
Size of population covered	10
Historical or traditional boundaries	6
Don't know/other	4

Source: MORI, December 1993

29   Figures 8 and 9 summarise the key findings on community identity of MORI's
County Durham survey. The general pattern of community identity found in the
other English counties is not mirrored in County Durham. Figure 8 shows that,
throughout County Durham, community affiliation is generally strongest in respect
of the local neighbourhood or village. The percentage of respondents identifying with
the county was, however, markedly higher than elsewhere at 84 per cent (very/fairly
strongly).

Figure 8

COMMUNITY IDENTITY IN COUNTY DURHAM: AN OVERVIEW

Question: 'How strongly do you feel you belong to each of the following areas?'

Percentage of respondents

	Very strongly	Very or fairly strongly
This neighbourhood/village	56	83
Town/nearest town	39	66
District/borough/city council area	37	68
County Durham	59	84

Source: MORI June/July 1993

THE LOCAL GOVERNMENT COMMISSION FOR ENGLAND

Figure 9

COMMUNITY IDENTITY IN COUNTY DURHAM

Question: 'How strongly do you feel you belong to each of the following areas?'

Percentage of respondents answering 'very or fairly strongly'

Authority	Neighbour-hood/ village	Town/ nearest town	District/borough/ city council/ area	County Durham
Chester-le-Street	80	77	73	86
Darlington	85	70	69	77
Derwentside	86	81	82	88
Durham City	84	78	70	87
Easington	83	41	58	85
Sedgefield	75	61	51	81
Teesdale	90	55	82	82
Wear Valley	85	67	71	83

Source: MORI, June/July 1992

30 Figure 9 illustrates the variation, by district, of community affiliations. The key points to emerge are:

(i) The sense of belonging to the county is least pronounced in Darlington (77 per cent, very/fairly strongly).

(ii) People in Derwentside tend to identify strongly with all areas.

(iii) Identification with the district area is lowest in Sedgefield (51 per cent) and highest in Teesdale and Derwentside (both 82 per cent).

31 The Commission regards these findings as important indicators of community identities and our recommendations have regard to the findings of this survey. In terms of local government structure (both the existing two-tier structure and any new unitary structure) the findings support the Commission's view, expressed in earlier reviews, and in its report, *Renewing Local Government in the English Shires*, that there is a need to devolve as much day-to-day management responsibility as possible to the community level and a need to provide an enhanced consultative role for parish and town councils.

32 Community identity must, however, be balanced against other considerations, such as the need to secure convenient and effective local government, and to have regard to the financial implications of any change.

3 THE STRUCTURAL OPTIONS FOR COUNTY DURHAM

33 The local authorities in County Durham have considered a number of options – both in the first review and the second review. They have continued to give a great deal of very helpful information to the Commission which wishes to acknowledge their work in producing submissions and their continuing support and co-operation.

34 The following preferences were put forward by the existing authorities in County Durham in the first review.

Figure 10
LOCAL AUTHORITY PREFERENCES: FIRST REVIEW

Authority	Preferences
Durham County Council	A single unitary authority or the retention of the two-tier system for the whole county are considered to be the only viable options.
Chester-le-Street	Regards a unitary county solution as 'the worst possible option'. The first choice of the authority is for a unitary district, its second choice is a merger of Chester-le-Street, Derwentside and Durham City, and its third choice would be for the retention of the existing two-tier system.
Darlington	Supports a unitary authority based on the existing borough boundary. Would prefer a unitary structure for the rest of County Durham.
Derwentside	Regards a unitary county solution as being devoid of community identity. The authority's first choice is for a unitary district and its second choice is for a merger with Chester-le-Street and Durham City.
Durham City	Most strongly opposes a unitary county solution. Preferred option is a unitary district. No other preferences were expressed in its Stage 3 submission.
Easington	Strongly supportive of a unitary district solution.
Sedgefield	Continues to regard a unitary district solution as the best option. It also argues that it would be willing to accept a merger with the neighbouring districts of Teesdale and Wear Valley, or the retention of the two-tier system.
Teesdale	Supports any option which will retain a principal authority based on the existing boundaries of Teesdale District, ie a unitary district solution or the retention of the existing two-tier system.
Wear Valley	Supports as its first preference a unitary authority based on the existing district. Has also identified a merger option which is not supported by any of the other districts, with Teesdale District, those parts of Sedgefield District to the west of the A1M motorway and those parts of Derwentside District to the west of the A68.

Source: Local authority submissions in the first review

35 The authorities have reconsidered their preferences as part of the second review. The preferences expressed by local authorities in the second review are set out in figure 11.

Figure 11
LOCAL AUTHORITY PREFERENCES: SECOND REVIEW

Authority	Preferences
Durham County Council, Chester-le-Street District, Darlington Borough, Durham City, Teesdale District	Unitary Darlington and status quo in the rest of the county.
Derwentside District, Easington District, Sedgefield District, Wear Valley District	Four unitary authorities (Darlington; Derwentside and Chester-le-Street; Easington and Durham City; and Sedgefield, Wear Valley and Teesdale)

Source: Local authority submissions

Note: Durham City Council submitted a second preference for five unitary authorities, which includes an expanded Durham City.

THE PROPOSAL FOR UNITARY DARLINGTON

36 Each of the principal authorities in County Durham has put forward a structural option for the area which includes a unitary authority for Darlington on its existing borough boundaries. The Commission believes that there are sound reasons for this.

(i) In the community identity survey undertaken by MORI in July 1992, 48 per cent of Darlington respondents identified very strongly with the borough council area, compared to a county-wide average of 37 per cent. Identification with County Durham was lower than in any other district area.

(ii) Darlington is based on a former county borough, although it does have a rural hinterland which is a catchment area in terms of work and shopping. Its travel-to-work area includes parts of neighbouring Teesdale and North Yorkshire.

(iii) Darlington lies on the axis between the North-South rail and road links and those going eastward into Teesside. The Borough Council argues that the current two-tier arrangements fail to recognise this position and there is 'little doubt about the "marginalisation" of Darlington by County Durham.' Darlington shares with Hartlepool, Middlesbrough and Stockton a dependence on the infrastructure based on Tees Port, the A66-A1 road connection, the East Coast main line railway and Teesside International Airport (whose site lies within both Darlington and Stockton boroughs).

37 The population of Darlington is approximately 100,000, which is below the indicative range for unitary authorities set out in the Commission's report, *Renewing Local Government in the English Shires*. However, on balance, the Commission judges that the authority would be able to provide the full range of local government services, albeit with recourse to joint arrangements with its Durham and Teesside neighbours. The new authority would be able to develop appropriate partnerships to reflect more accurately the needs and community identities of its citizens.

38 Estimates of the financial effects of moving to unitary structures have been prepared for the county area as a whole. The extent of any savings/costs arising from a new unitary authority for Darlington would depend on what was adopted for the rest of the county area. The Commission's initial estimates of annual savings/costs, as well as the costs of change, are set out in Appendix A.

COUNTY DURHAM OUTSIDE DARLINGTON

39 In its original review, the Commission considered a single unitary structure for the whole of the county area. However, because of the strong case for Darlington to become a new unitary authority, which has the support of all principal authorities in County Durham, the Commission does not feel able to put this option forward for further consideration.

40 The Commission has looked again at alternative structures for the rest of the county, outside Darlington, as follows:

(i) a single unitary authority;

(ii) seven unitary authorities;

(iii) three unitary authorities, as set out in the submission prepared jointly by Derwentside, Easington, Sedgefield and Wear Valley District Councils;

(iv) retention of the existing two-tier arrangements, as recommended in the Commission's report to the Secretary of State in November 1993.

41 The Commission has carefully weighed the advantages and disadvantages of each of these before drawing its own conclusions.

A SINGLE UNITARY AUTHORITY OUTSIDE DARLINGTON

42 The community identity survey undertaken by MORI indicates that across the review area 59 per cent of respondents identify very strongly with County Durham which compares with an average of only 12 per cent across the counties in the first tranche of reviews. The differential between those identifying very strongly with County Durham and those identifying very strongly with the district council area is 22 per cent, which is also in sharp contrast to the results for the other counties in the first tranche of reviews.

43 Notwithstanding the very high level of identity with County Durham – which enjoys greater public support than any other county in shire England – the county outside Darlington is not homogeneous. There are contrasts between the rugged beauty of the Pennines in the west and the industrialised parts of the county in Consett and Easington, and again the rich cultural inheritance at Chester-le-Street and Durham City, the latter being a world heritage site. However, communities within the county area share common characteristics. There is a shared industrial heritage with the wealth of the county having been built on iron, steel and coal. This is now giving way to other economic activity such as light engineering and the service sector. Agriculture continues to be significant, particularly in the west of the county. Much of the county has some form of assisted area status reflecting the continuing economic challenges being faced. The existence of a large authority would allow flexibility in channelling resources into areas of greatest need.

44 A unitary authority serving a population of approximately half a million would be self-sufficient in all major services. There would therefore be no need for joint arrangements with the new Darlington authority, except for those relating to the police and fire services. There would be no difficulty in recruiting specialist staff. Moreover, the Commission's estimate of the financial consequences of establishing a structure of two unitary authorities – one for Darlington and one for the rest of the county – is that there would be annual savings in administrative expenditure in the range of £9 million to £14 million.

45 On the other hand, such an authority would have to overcome problems of perceived remoteness. This was one of the major concerns expressed by those attending public meetings held in May and June 1993.

46 In weighing up the available evidence, the Commission must consider the expressed preferences of people in the review area. In the public consultation exercise, which was undertaken as part of the original review from 10 May 1993 to 10 July 1993, 29 per cent of respondents expressed a preference for a two unitary authority structure. However, the proportion of respondents outside Darlington supporting this option was lower, at approximately 20 per cent. In the independent survey undertaken by MORI on behalf of the Commission during July and August 1993, only 9 per cent of respondents county-wide cited the two unitary option as their preference. This ranged from 31 per cent in Darlington to only 1 per cent in Chester-le-Street.

47 This indicates that, while there may be good service delivery and cost effectiveness reasons why a two unitary authority structure would be viable, this is clearly not a structure which commands support amongst local people. It is therefore not one which the Commission considers it should put forward again for public consultation.

SEVEN UNITARY AUTHORITIES OUTSIDE DARLINGTON

48 The district councils in Durham originally expressed a preference for unitary status on their existing district boundaries. The Commission assessed this structure as part of the original review and concluded that it could not recommend such a structure.

49 The Commission did not consider that the resulting authorities would be able to deliver the full range of local government services. There would be a proliferation of joint arrangements which would be fragile because of the number of partners involved. Authorities would find it difficult to recruit and retain specialist staff and there would be a serious risk of services being jeopardised. During the transitional period there would be substantial disruption to county level services, and to community care arrangements in particular. Further, a unitary district structure did not provide a good 'fit' with the evidence about community identity. Finally, such a structure would cost significantly more than the existing two-tier system and the costs of transition to such a new structure would never be recovered.

50 The Commission's views were supported by many of those consulted in the earlier review. National and regional organisations, as well as business organisations, opposed a move to a large number of smaller unitary authorities. Of the 27,900 people who wrote directly to the Commission during the nine week consultation period which started on 10 May 1993, only approximately 12 per cent favoured a unitary district option. The MORI survey indicated that, overall, only 7 per cent of respondents supported an eight unitary authority option. This ranged from 12 per cent in Darlington to 4 per cent in Derwentside and Durham City.

51 Taking all the evidence into account the Commission re-affirms its original conclusion that a unitary district option should not be considered further.

THREE UNITARY AUTHORITIES OUTSIDE DARLINGTON

52 During the second stage of the original review, the Durham branch of the Association of District Councils (ADC) put forward an option consisting of four unitary authorities based on mergers of Chester-le-Street, Derwentside and Durham City; and Sedgefield, Teesdale and Wear Valley; with Easington and Darlington on their existing boundaries. The Commission considered then that this option could not be

put forward for public consultation as it did not meet the criteria of the 1992 Act. The subsequent evidence confirmed that this option did not command local support. Less than 1 per cent of those writing directly to the Commission expressed a preference for unitary authorities based on merged districts and the option also registered only a small measure of support in the MORI survey (10 per cent overall as a first preference).

53   However a more recent submission, *Four for the Future*, jointly prepared by Derwentside, Easington, Sedgefield and Wear Valley District Councils, puts forward a different configuration of mergers to create three unitary authorities outside Darlington, as set out in map 2 and figure 12 below. Unfortunately, in each merger one of the potential partners is opposed to the idea.

Figure 12
FOUR UNITARY AUTHORITIES

Authority	Constituent areas	Population	Area (ha)	Density (Pop/ha)
Darlington	Darlington Borough Council	100,100	19,800	5.1
North Durham	Chester-le-Street and Derwentside District Councils	140,100	33,900	4.1
Durham	Durham City and Easington District Councils	187,200	33,300	5.6
South West Durham	Sedgefield, Teesdale and Wear Valley District Councils	179,600	156,400	1.1

Sources: OPCS mid-1992 estimates for population figures; Municipal Yearbook 1994 for area.

54   The **Durham Council** would be based on the city of Durham and the towns of Peterlee and Seaham. The hinterland shares similar characteristics: it is constituted of former colliery villages and small agricultural settlements. Although the coal industry has all but disappeared, it is still a part of the proud tradition of the area. However, most markedly in Easington, the industry has also left a legacy of environmental problems, derelict land and unemployment. The city of Durham provides a sharp contrast, being a centre for tourism, shopping, education and service industries. The city acts as a magnet for shopping and leisure activities, but road links between Easington and the city are not particularly strong. Easington has an outflow of workers to Sunderland and Hartlepool, which exert as much of an influence over Easington as does Durham City.

Map 2
FOUR UNITARY AUTHORITIES

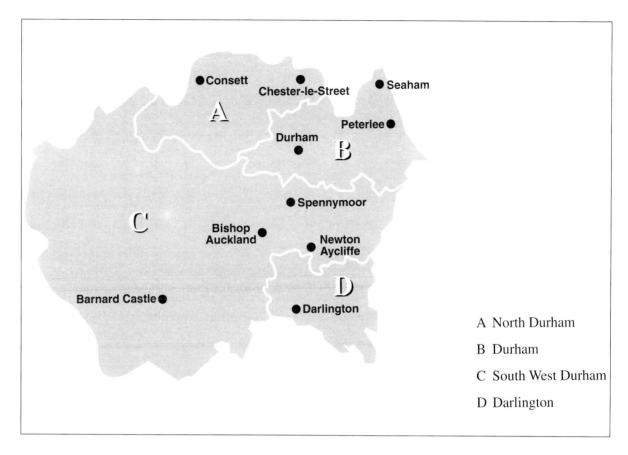

A North Durham

B Durham

C South West Durham

D Darlington

55   Durham City Council, which opposes such a merger, in a letter of clarification dated
     31 May 1994, summarises the contrast as follows:

     'To pretend that there is a commonality of character or purpose between
     the two areas could only blur the focus that will be required to overcome
     these [economic] difficulties.

     'The people of Peterlee look upon a visit to Durham City as a day out. This
     is not the stuff upon which to construct a cohesive unit of local
     government.'

56   The **North Durham authority** would be based on the towns of Chester-le-Street,
     Consett and Stanley. The area is affected by its proximity to the Tyneside
     conurbation, which is a major source of jobs and recreational/shopping facilities for
     residents. Links between the districts of Chester-le-Street (whose council favours the
     continuation of the present two-tier arrangements) and Derwentside are less
     pronounced. The Derwentside area is facing major economic regeneration and is still
     coping with the aftermath of the closure of the Consett steelworks in 1980. (These
     problems are similar to those previously faced in Sedgefield with the closure of the
     Shildon coachworks and those being addressed now in Easington with the closure of
     the 'super pits' on the coast).

57 The **South West Durham authority** would include the towns of Barnard Castle, Bishop Auckland, Crook, Newton Aycliffe and Spennymoor. Much of the authority would be sparsely populated in the rural west of the county, where the district council (Teesdale) is not in favour of the proposed merger. Weardale and Teesdale residents' patterns of shopping and leisure are focused on the towns of Bishop Auckland and Barnard Castle respectively. Although the two valleys share the same rural characteristics, they are cut off from one another by moorland which is only crossed by a few very minor roads. When residents venture further afield, for example for household shopping, it tends to be to Darlington. There are contrasting characteristics in the east and west of the proposed authority. The boundaries between Wear Valley and Sedgefield are blurred, with travel-to-work areas overlapping around Bishop Auckland, Shildon and Newton Aycliffe.

58 The four unitary authorities would 'nest' within the Training and Enterprise Council boundaries, and there would be a match within health authority boundaries, except for the Durham council which would need to liaise with the North Durham, Sunderland and Hartlepool Health Authorities.

59 The MORI survey on community identity did not ask about identification with these combined areas. In terms of expressed preferences from residents, reference has already been made to the results of the previous Stage 3 consultation exercise where there was little support for merged districts. The Commission has only heard from a very small number of residents in Stage 1 of the second review. This has not provided any indication of there being a groundswell of support for the proposed mergers. National and regional organisations, including those representing businesses, have voiced disquiet about any local government structure which resulted in the loss of the county council. There is no local consensus among local authorities for this option, as there is an unwilling partner in each merger.

60 In terms of service delivery, the proposed authorities would be large enough to deliver the majority of local government services. Joint arrangements would be necessary in any sub-county option, but here they would be limited mainly to those associated with law and order related services, strategic planning, highways, transportation and economic development, and those areas where it is more effective to organise on a county-wide basis (for example archive provision). There is a risk, however, that a strategic response to the very serious social and economic regeneration problems faced in County Durham might be lost if the county were to be broken up into four pieces. In the transitional period there would be disruption to both county and district services.

61 The joint submission from the four districts includes an estimate of the financial consequences of change to a four unitary authority structure. This indicates that annual savings of over £9 million might be achieved, recovering transitional costs of £23 million within three years. The Commission has undertaken its own assessment which is set out in Appendix A. The Commission estimates that annual savings would be more modest, in the range of £2 million to £6 million a year, with transitional costs of between £19 million and £22 million.

62 The Commission has carefully weighed the advantages and disadvantages of this option, and has concluded that it cannot recommend a four unitary authority structure to local people because it fails, comprehensively, to meet the requirements of the 1992 Act, and the Government's Guidance to the Commission.

RETENTION OF THE EXISTING TWO-TIER SYSTEM OUTSIDE DARLINGTON

63 The Commission's final recommendation to the Secretary of State in November 1993 was for a unitary authority based on Darlington Borough Council with no change to the rest of the county area. As figure 11 shows, this now has the support of five of the nine local authorities in County Durham, including Durham County Council. It is also supported by all the Members of Parliament in County Durham.

64 This structure would also reflect the community identity findings in the MORI survey, which shows that 84 per cent of respondents identify very or fairly strongly with County Durham: significantly more than identify with their nearest town or district council area. It would also acknowledge the stronger sense of identity in Darlington with the borough council area.

65 The current division of services between the county council and the districts would remain (outside Darlington), with the county council being responsible for most schools and other aspects of education, social services, libraries, trading standards, highways and transport, police and fire services. The district councils would continue to be responsible for housing, most planning decisions, environmental services (including refuse collection), and leisure and recreational facilities. An indication of the different functions has been provided already in figure 2.

66 There are a number of advantages in retaining the two-tier system. The bulk of local government services in terms of volume of expenditure is already provided by the county tier of the two-tier system. Retention of the system would avoid the costs of change and any disruption to services. Established links with other public and private bodies and organisations such as health authorities, the Training and Enterprise Council and economic development partnerships would be maintained. Retention of the two-tier arrangements would also maintain the ability to manage strategic issues while providing for local identity. These benefits would not be significantly diminished by Darlington becoming a unitary authority.

67   The authorities promoting this option have put considerable effort into proposals to modify and improve the present arrangements and, in so doing, address some of the perceived weaknesses of the two-tier system. They argue that there are practical ways to overcome the confusion and duplication that now exists between the two tiers. These include better co-operation between authorities, delegation of functions, agency agreements and, for example, the development of joint information and assistance points for the public.

68   The creation of a unitary authority for Darlington and no change elsewhere in the county area would reflect the views expressed to the Commission, both in the large scale public consultation exercise lasting for nine weeks from 10 May 1993, and in the (very modest) level of response that we have received since the second review began. The former showed that almost half of respondents supported the retention of the status quo, although there was very strong support for a unitary authority based on the borough area in Darlington. Of more recent respondents, 45 per cent wish to see retention of the two-tier system, and most of those who support a sub-county option call only for a unitary Darlington and a two-tier system in the rest of the county.

69   It is also important to consider the MORI findings which show that, unlike in most other counties subject to review, the majority of respondents in County Durham are opposed to unitary authorities in principle. Forty-seven per cent of respondents oppose the principle, compared to 39 per cent who support it. The strong exception to the overall pattern is Darlington where 74 per cent of respondents support the principle. The same trend is discernible in the results of the survey when questions are asked about actual unitary structures. Overall, 56 per cent of respondents supported the existing arrangements as their first preference. In every district the existing two-tier system was the most popular choice as first preference, except for Darlington where unitary structures involving a unitary Darlington were supported by 65 per cent of respondents compared to 23 per cent who preferred the status quo.

*   *   *

70   The Commission is cautious about the likelihood of structures succeeding which do not have local support. It considers that the message from its various consultation exercises is unambiguous. The Commission therefore proposes to put forward for consultation a draft recommendation that there should be a unitary authority for the borough area of Darlington, and that the existing two-tier arrangements should continue in the rest of the county. It is not putting forward any other alternatives, for the reasons stated above.

DRAFT RECOMMENDATION

There should be a new unitary authority based on the present borough area of Darlington.

There should be no change to the existing two-tier arrangements in the rest of the Durham County Council area.

4   OTHER MATTERS

71   In addition to looking at the structure of local authorities in County Durham, the Commission is also required to examine the position of individual services, to make recommendations about future electoral arrangements and to take account of the part that town and parish councils could play in each area it reviews. These matters are covered below.

PUBLIC PROTECTION (POLICE, FIRE AND OTHER SERVICES RELATED TO LAW AND ORDER)

72   The Government's guidance to the Commission on police and fire services is explicit in requiring them to be carried out over an area no smaller than at present. As a separate exercise, in which the Commission is not involved, the Government is developing new proposals for police authorities, the probation service and magistrates' courts. In the meantime, the Commission recommends that the public protection and the law and order services should continue to cover the present county area of County Durham and that joint authorities should be established for these services on which representatives of the appropriate new councils should serve.

DRAFT RECOMMENDATION

There should be a combined authority established in the present County Durham area for each of the police and fire services, on which representatives of Durham County Council and a new unitary Darlington Council would serve. No changes are proposed to the probation and magistrates' courts services.

STRATEGIC PLANNING

73   The Commission is concerned that strategic land use planning for County Durham should not be undermined by changes in the structure of local authorities. This matter is fully discussed in the Commission's report, *Renewing Local Government in the English Shires*. As the present authorities recognise, there is a high level of interdependence between different parts of the county and this needs to be reflected in an appropriate planning structure. The Commission is invited by the legislation to consider whether unitary authorities should be empowered to prepare unitary development plans rather than, as at present, structure plans and local plans.

74 The Commission considers that there is a need for the existing structure planning and local planning systems to be maintained across the area of County Durham (outside Darlington) as it exists at present. As far as Darlington is concerned the Commission wishes to re-affirm its earlier proposal that the area of the new unitary authority should form part of a joint structure plan for the Tees Valley sub region which incorporates the four proposed Cleveland unitary authorities.

DRAFT RECOMMENDATION

Darlington should assume joint responsibility for structure planning with the proposed unitary authorities of Hartlepool, Middlesbrough, Redcar and East Cleveland and Stockton-on-Tees for the whole of their combined areas. The joint structure plan would include strategic waste and minerals planning. Darlington should have individual responsibility for formulating detailed minerals and waste policies in its area in general conformity with the policy framework established by the structure plan, and should exercise development control functions for all purposes. There should be no change in the allocation of land-use planning functions in the remainder of County Durham.

OTHER SERVICES

75 The Commission acknowledges that the case of Darlington is special in that it looks not only to the Tees Valley but also north to the rest of County Durham. The Commission believes that the new unitary authority it proposes will command sufficient resources for it to carry out the main local government services, whether directly or by 'contracting out' their provision, either to other local authorities (within County Durham or elsewhere) or to the private sector. The Commission expects the new authority to take steps to ensure that specialist expertise is not unnecessarily broken up and that the existing levels of efficiency and effectiveness in the provision of relatively small-scale but important functions, such as trading standards, archive provision and emergency planning, are maintained.

ELECTORAL ARRANGEMENTS

76 The Commission has examined the means by which local democratic control and accountability can be secured within the new structure. The present electoral arrangements in County Durham create a certain amount of confusion in that some councils hold elections most years (elections by thirds) whereas the others have elections for the whole council every four years. In addition, accountability is blurred by the fact that some wards return either two or three councillors. The Commission

generally supports the view of the Committee of Inquiry into the Conduct of Local Authority Business (1986) that there should be one councillor for every electoral ward and that the whole council should be elected together once every four years.

77 The Commission's report, *Renewing Local Government in the English Shires*, sets out the Commission's view that the ratio of councillors to local residents should generally be around 1 to 4,000. This ratio is midway between the existing ratios for district and for county councils and in line with that for the existing metropolitan districts, the only unitary authorities in England outside London. It also reflects the Commission's wish to see both a different role for councillors and that more backup and support should be made available to assist them in carrying out their difficult task. However, it is not a hard and fast rule and the Commission wishes to apply it sensitively, taking into account sparsely populated areas, or particularly deprived areas, as well as the need to minimise disruption.

78 The Commission proposes to review electoral arrangements generally throughout England during the next five years. In County Durham, that review will be able to look further at the local authority electoral arrangements. In the meantime, the Commission wishes to re-affirm its earlier recommendation that there should be no change to the electoral and warding arrangements for the remaining seven district councils, nor to present arrangements for the Durham County Council area outside Darlington.

DRAFT RECOMMENDATION

The new unitary authority for Darlington should continue with the present borough electoral and warding arrangements. There should be no change to the present electoral and warding arrangements for the remaining seven Durham districts, nor to the present arrangements for Durham County Council outside Darlington.

79 Details of the existing electoral arrangements are set out in Appendix B for information.

LOCAL COUNCILS

80 The Commission considers that the structure of local government in County Durham should build on the strong sense of identity with immediate neighbourhoods, as found by the MORI survey.

81 Since parish and town councils can be an important reflection of that sense of identity within the community, the Commission recommends that their role should be enhanced. This should include regular meetings with the principal local authorities, improved consultation on planning and highways issues and – where there is a

demand from a local council – devolved management of local facilities like sports grounds and libraries. Members of parish and town councils would also be well placed to help residents secure assistance or redress when faced with problems regarding local services. These proposals enlarge on existing practice and reflect suggestions in many of the submissions to the Commission, both nationally and locally.

82 Neither the Government nor the Commission envisages an increase in the statutory powers of parish and town councils, nor the establishment of another tier of local government – few respondents have argued for this. However, the Commission does see an important role for parish and town councils in empowering local communities. The Commission agrees with many of its respondents that a clear consultative framework should be established between local authorities and parish and town councils. This framework, or 'local charter', could ensure that parish and town councils have rights to the following:

(i) a clear statement of those matters affecting the local community upon which they will be consulted, with the areas for consultation being widely drawn;

(ii) sufficient information from principal authorities about local matters on which local councils' views have been requested;

(iii) the right to a written explanation from a principal authority if it decides, as it legitimately may, not to agree with the views of the parish or town council;

(iv) regular meetings between representatives of the principal authority and the parish and town councils to discuss matters of common interest.

83 The Commission has received sufficient evidence from residents of the Haswell parish in the district of Easington proposing that the parish be divided into two (based on the settlements of Haswell and South Hetton to reflect more closely the two community identities), for it to consult on this particular issue and make the following draft recommendation. (Further details appear in Appendix C.)

DRAFT RECOMMENDATION

The existing parish of Haswell should be abolished, and should be replaced by two parishes:

(i) a parish area covering the district ward of Haswell;

(ii) a parish area covering the district ward of South Hetton.

84 In addition, there have been a number of representations for emparishment of unparished areas of County Durham. Submissions requesting emparishment were received from local people in the following areas:

(i) Bishop Auckland

(ii) Binchester

(iii) Coundon

(iv) Crook

(v) Dene Valley

(vi) Six unparished Durham City Council wards: Framwellgate, Elvet, Pelaw, Newton Hall, Nevilles Cross and Gilesgate.

(vii) Escombe and Witton Park

(viii) Hunwick

(ix) Newfield

(x) Willington

(xi) Witton-le-Wear

85 The cases for emparishment were generally well argued, but there was not sufficient evidence of extensive public interest or support. It has not been possible to carry out a detailed review within the statutory timetable for the structural review and therefore a future boundary and electoral review of the area will be needed.

DRAFT RECOMMENDATION

If there is clear local support for parishing areas in County Durham which are not currently parished, the Secretary of State should be invited to direct the Commission to undertake a review in which the scope for future parishing can be considered.

In addition, there should be an enhanced consultative role for all town and parish councils.

Elections for parish and town councils should, wherever possible, be held at the same time as elections for the principal authorities.

5   NEXT STEPS

86   The Commission has again put forward a draft recommendation for the future structure of local government in County Durham which would leave the existing two-tier arrangements in place, with the exception of a unitary authority in Darlington. Once more, it is up to the people of the area. The Commission wishes to take local representations fully into account. It would like to receive them by 26 September 1994. Representations received after this date may not be taken into account by the Commission, and all representations will be available for public inspection by appointment after 10 October 1994. You should express your views by writing directly to the Commission at the address below:

> Durham Review
> Local Government Commission for England
> Dolphyn Court
> 10-11 Great Turnstile
> Lincoln's Inn Fields
> London
> WC1V 7JU

The Commission regrets that it will not be able to acknowledge your letter.

87   The Commission will consider reactions from all those with a stake in local government in County Durham, and will review its draft recommendations to see whether they should be altered before reporting finally to the Secretary of State for the Environment later in the year. The Secretary of State will then decide whether to support the recommendations, and to lay the necessary regulations before Parliament in order to implement any changes.

APPENDIX A

FINANCIAL COMPARISONS

The Commission is required to consider the change in overhead costs which may result from changes in the structure of local government. This is not a straightforward matter and the issues concerned are discussed more fully in the Commission's report, *Renewing Local Government in the English Shires*.

Figure A1 shows the existing local government indirect expenditure (administrative overheads) based upon financial material provided by the local authorities in County Durham. The Government's guidance asks the Commission to look only at indirect expenditure, which typically represents about 10 per cent of total local government spending.

Figure A2 shows the Commission's estimates of annual savings and transitional costs for each structural option.

Figure A1
ESTIMATE OF EXISTING LOCAL GOVERNMENT INDIRECT SPENDING

	£million
Staff costs (including associated overheads)	55
Accommodation	4
Information Technology	8
Democracy	2
Total indirect costs	69

Source: Local Government Commission

Figure A2

COMPARISON OF THE INDIRECT COSTS OF THE STRUCTURAL OPTIONS
AGAINST EXISTING ARRANGEMENTS

Option	Annual savings/ costs £million	Transitional costs £million	Payback period years
Unitary Darlington and two-tier rest of county	From £2m cost to £1m saving	From £1m to £5m	Five years or, in the worst case, never
Four unitary districts (ADC's second review proposal)	From £2m to £6m saving	From £19m to £24m	Under 4 years to 12 years

Source: Local Government Commission

Note: The base data was that used in the earlier review. Because of time constraints,
principal authorities did not undertake a review of the 1993/94 status quo indirect costs
and did not carry out a detailed financial appraisal. The Commission agrees with this
approach and has therefore also used 1992/93 as the base year.

The county and district councils in County Durham provided their own estimates of the
financial consequences of a range of structural alternatives. However, in order to secure a
consistent approach, the Commission applied the Ernst & Young financial methodology
to produce the financial estimates set out in Figure A2. These figures may differ from
those produced by the local authorities. For example, the Commission's assumptions
about the staffing requirements of new authorities may differ from those of the local
authorities. The figures are expressed as a range to reflect the broad nature of the
estimates and assumptions involved.

APPENDIX B

ELECTORAL ARRANGEMENTS

EXISTING ELECTORAL ARRANGEMENTS

This appendix contains a summary of the existing electoral arrangements in County Durham. It should be noted that the electoral arrangements throughout the review area should be subject to full review in due course.

The proposed new unitary authority for Darlington will have the same number of councillors (52) as the present borough council, and there will be no change to the electoral arrangements of the seven district councils outside Darlington. The county council will have 61 members in 61 divisions outside Darlington, as at present.

Figure B1
EXISTING DISTRICT ELECTORAL ARRANGEMENTS.

Principal authority	Electorate	Wards	Number of councillors	Councillor-to-elector ratio
Chester-le-Street	42,019	17	33	1:1,273
Darlington	76,867	25	52	1:1,478
Derwentside	69,189	23	55	1:1,258
Durham City	68,924	24	49	1:1,407
Easington	76,161	26	51	1:1,493
Sedgefield	69,857	22	49	1:1,426
Teesdale	19,629	19	31	1:633
Wear Valley	49,842	21	40	1:1,246
Total	472,488	177	360	1:1,312

Source: Pre-submission data from the councils concerned

Figure B2

EXISTING COUNTY ELECTORAL ARRANGEMENTS

District area	Electorate	Divisions	Number of Councillors	Councillor-to-elector ratio
Chester-le-Street	42,019	6	6	1:7,003
Darlington	76,867	11	11	1:6,987
Derwentside	69,189	11	11	1:6,290
Durham City	68,924	10	10	1:6,892
Easington	76,161	12	12	1:6,924
Sedgefield	69,857	11	11	1:6,351
Teesdale	19,629	3	3	1:6,543
Wear Valley	49,842	8	8	1:6,230
Durham County Council	472,488	72	72	1:6,562

Source: Pre-submission data from the councils concerned

THE LOCAL GOVERNMENT COMMISSION FOR ENGLAND

APPENDIX C

PROPOSED PARISHING ARRANGEMENTS

HASWELL

Haswell parish area currently covers two district wards which correspond to the two settlements of South Hetton and Haswell. The Commission has received a petition bearing approximately 350 signatures, as well as a number of individual letters, requesting that the parish area be split into two parishes corresponding to the two district wards. The Commission wishes to know whether this proposal is more widely supported by the people of that area and invites views on the subject.

The boundary between the two parished areas would follow the existing district ward boundary as illustrated in map C1. The two parishes would be known as Haswell and South Hetton respectively.

There are currently nine parish councillors serving the present Haswell parish area. The Commission recommends that, should new parish councils be established for these two areas, initially there should be five parish councillors for the new Haswell parish serving an electorate of approximately 1,400, and six for the new South Hetton parish area serving an electorate of approximately 2,150. The electoral arrangements should be subject to review in due course.

Map C1

THE PROPOSED DIVISION OF HASWELL PARISH INTO TWO NEW
PARISHES

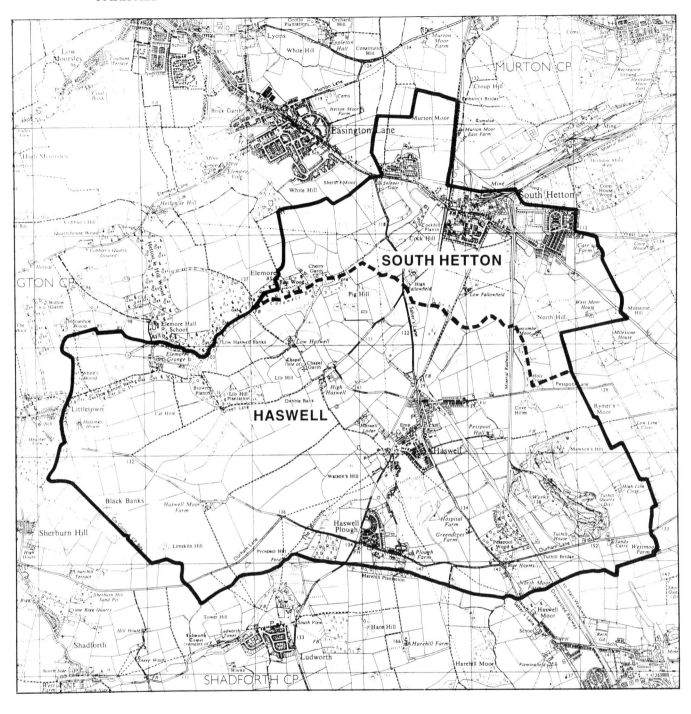

——————— Existing Parish Boundary

▬▬ ▬▬ ▬▬ Ward Boundary & Proposed Parish Boundary

Printed in the United Kingdom for HMSO
Dd. 0296879, C31, 6/94, 3400, 291657

THE LOCAL GOVERNMENT COMMISSION FOR ENGLAND